Second Edition

Before Book One

Listening Activities
for Prebeginning
Students of English

John R. Boyd · Mary Ann Boyd

PRENTICE HALL REGENTS
Englewood Cliffs, New Jersey 07632

Editorial / Production supervision and interior design: Noël Vreeland Carter
Aquisitions editor: Anne Riddick
Cover design: Bruce Kenselaar
Interior art coordination: Karen Noferi and Noël Vreeland Carter
Pre-press buyer: Ray Keating
Manufacturing buyer: Lori Bulwin
Scheduler: Leslie Coward

Illustrations by: Len Shalansky
Additional drawings by: Erasmo Hernandez
Photography by: Jane Latta

© 1991, 1982 by Prentice-Hall, Inc.
A Division of Simon & Schuster
Englewood Cliffs, New Jersey 07632

Printed in the United States of America

10 9 8 7 6 5

0-13-068289-6

Prentice-Hall International (UK) Limited, *London*
Prentice-Hall of Australia Pty. Limited, *Sydney*
Prentice-Hall Canada Inc., *Toronto*
Prentice-Hall Hispanoamericana, S.A., *Mexico*
Prentice-Hall of India Private Limited, *New Delhi*
Prentice-Hall of Japan, Inc., *Tokyo*
Simon & Schuster Asia Pte., *Singapore*
Editora Prentice-Hall do Brasil, Ltda., *Rio de Janiero*

Introduction

Most texts that are labeled "beginning" presuppose some familiarity with spoken English. However, many beginning students are zero-level speakers of English and have not been exposed to the language—have not heard enough of it—to be able to produce English sounds. Students who enter the beginning level ESL class unfamiliar with the sounds of the language are ill-equipped to succeed in the task of learning to speak English. Too often, within the beginning class, these students will be pushed into speaking before their listening skills have been developed. This inability to comprehend aurally will impede the ability to respond orally. Unable to produce oral language, the students find failure, which increases the anxiety which they already naturally feel in the language classroom. However, if oral production can be delayed until the students acquire rudimentary aural comprehension, the probability of their achieving oral proficiency is increased.

Before Book One is based on the philosophy that the ability to listen to the sounds of English, comprehend them, and demonstrate that comprehension nonverbally is a prerequisite to mastering oral communication skills. Moreover, much of the English language lends itself to a primarily—if not exclusively—aural presentation. Therefore, the activities of the book, although predominantly centered on listening and nonverbal responding, are set in true communicative frameworks. For example, being able to hear and write down a telephone number given orally is a true communicative act and one of the goals of Unit One.

Many of the first activities found in the book revolve around numbers. There are several reasons for choosing numbers. They include the following:

1. numbers are a universal feature of human experience and thus of language;
2. the meaning of numbers is immediately comprehended;
3. the names of the numbers are relatively easy to master aurally;
4. numbers provide a useful foundation for subsequent language learning activities; and
5. students seem to enjoy learning and using numbers.

Before Book One is an appropriate first text for students from any first language background who enter an ESL class without prior study or exposure to English. No one is at too low a level to use the material. It can be, and has been, used at the junior high, high school and adult levels both within a class and in a one-on-one tutoring session. Because it sharpens aural skills while easing students into the language learning environment, it can serve as introductory text to any ESL or literacy series.

In the nearly ten years since the initial publication of *Before Book One*, the philosophy that it espouses has been verified again and again both by our students themselves and by our colleagues. However, over these intervening years, our perception of the audience for whom the book is appropriate has broadened and now includes both students who lack familiarity with the Roman alphabet and those who are labelled "false beginners."

Although we still hold to our earlier statement that "no one is at too low a level to use the material," we now recognize that some students—illiterate or pre-literate in their native language—lack the familiarity with the Roman alphabet necessary to complete the dictation portion of each exercise unless they are given some additional preparation. For that reason we have included in Part 2 of the Appendix of this expanded second edition optional worksheets which introduce numbers and letters for tracing and practice by those students who may need this extra help.

As we have mentioned, in developing *Before Book One* we kept in mind an audience of "pre-beginning" students. Yet it has been called to our attention over the years that so-called "false-beginners" can gain much by beginning their classroom language instruction with this text. In his 1986 teacher resource text, *Images and Options in the Classroom,* published by Cambridge University Press, Earl W. Stevick devoted an entire chapter to the options available to the teacher for the successful use of *Before Book One* with students who may not be true zero-level students. We are grateful for his thorough discussion of *Before Book One* which has shown so many teachers the possibilities inherent in the text.

The detailed Teacher's Manual for *Before Book One* contains suggestions on how to introduce material as well as instructions for working through the activities within each unit. As such, it is an *essential* companion to the student book. It has been written as a how-to manual for the untrained teacher as well as a guide for the experienced teacher.

UNIT 1 NUMBERS AND LETTERS

PRACTICE A

	1	2	3	4	5

PART 1

1.	(334)	332	331
2.	221	(222)	225
3.	553	554	(551)
4.	112	(114)	113
5.	454	434	(424)
6.	312	213	(321)
7.	453	(345)	534
8.	(152)	215	521

PART 2

1.	2 2 4	6.	3 2 4
2.	3 3 1	7.	5 3 1
3.	4 4 2	8.	4 2 4
4.	1 1 3	9.	3 5 2
5.	2 2 5	10.	5 4 1

PRACTICE B

PART 1

1.	(556)	557	559
2.	666	669	(668)
3.	(776)	777	779
4.	889	(886)	888
5.	996	995	(998)
6.	376	367	(637)
7.	148	(814)	184
8.	694	(496)	469
9.	(842)	248	482
10.	639	369	(693)

PART 2

1. 768
2. 967
3. 878
4. 668
5. 788

6. 379
7. 811
8. 591
9. 765
10. 933

PRACTICE C

059 702 063 305 240

PART 1

1.	(104)	401	140
2.	120	210	201
3.	025	520	052
4.	507	570	750
5.	002	200	020
6.	9800	8900	8090
7.	3021	3201	2301
8.	6075	7605	6705
9.	4070	7400	7040
10.	9080	8090	9008

PART 2

1. _____		6. _____
2. _____		7. _____
3. _____		8. _____
4. _____		9. _____
5. _____		10. _____

3

PRACTICE D

RAFAEL CABRERA

1. 828-11_84

2. 452-63_29

3. 45_3_-0789

4. 354-29_4_3

5. _5_46-2237

6. 829-_66_35

7. 7_77_-6425

8. 691-_88_23

9. 574-33_99_

10. 991-2_100_0

---

1. 456-7_538_

2. 791-_344_4

3. 7_01_-_1_127

4. 68_7_-_89_99

5. 7_0_1-_1_362

6. 442-_1687_

7. 90_0_-_81_13

8. 831-_44 44_

9. 321-_8_55_2_

10. 2_05_-3_7_91

---

1. 77_5-1829_

2. 2_86_-_16 7_8

3. 3_91_-_53 2_1

4. 65_8-1137_

5. 8_17_-_19 4_2

6. _346-4020_

7. _625-2200_

8. _333-4692_

9. _838-3000_

10. _520-7090_

4

PRACTICE E   *RAFAEL CABRERA*

PART 1

| 1 A | 2 B | 3 C | 4 D | 5 E | 6 F | 7 G |

PART 2

	A	B	C
1.	AE	(BE)	DE
2.	(AD)	(AE)	AB
3.	(AGG)	EGG	CGG
4.	AFE	(ACE)	AGE
5.	(BEE)	BED	BEB
6.	(FEED)	BEED	CEED
7.	FAGE	FADE	(FACE)
8.	(CAGED)	CEGED	CAEED
9.	FACAD	FACEB	(FACED)
10.	(BAGGED)	BEGGED	BAGGAD

PART 3

1. *BE*
2. *ACE*
3. *BED*

4. *AGE*
5. *FADE*
6. *BEGGED*

PRACTICE E

PART 1

1	2	3	4	5	6	7	8	9
H	I	J	K	L	M	N	O	P

PART 2

	A	B	C
1.	IH	OH	EH
2.	NI	NO	NA
3.	JIM	PIM	HIM
4.	HIP	HOP	HAP
5.	MEN	MEM	MEE
6.	MILK	NILK	HILK
7.	JAEL	JAIL	JAOL
8.	KEEL	KEEN	KEEP
9.	POKED	PAKED	PIKED
10.	APPKE	APPLE	APPAE

PART 3

1. _____   4. _____

2. _____   5. _____

3. _____   6. _____

PRACTICE G

PART 1

1	2	3	4	5	6	7	8	9	10
Q	R	S	T	U	V	W	X	Y	Z

PART 2

	A	B	C
1.	TO	VO	ZO
2.	UZ	UX	US
3.	VRY	WRY	TRY
4.	OUT	OUR	OUQ
5.	ZUST	RUST	YUST
6.	QUIT	QUIZ	QUIX
7.	TROE	TRUE	TRWE
8.	ESTRA	EXTRA	EZTRA
9.	STERT	STURT	START
10.	TWEST	TWIST	TWUST

PART 3

1. _____
2. _____
3. _____
4. _____
5. _____
6. _____

PRACTICE **H**

11 12 13 14 15 16 17 18 19 20 21

PART 1

A   **B**   **C**

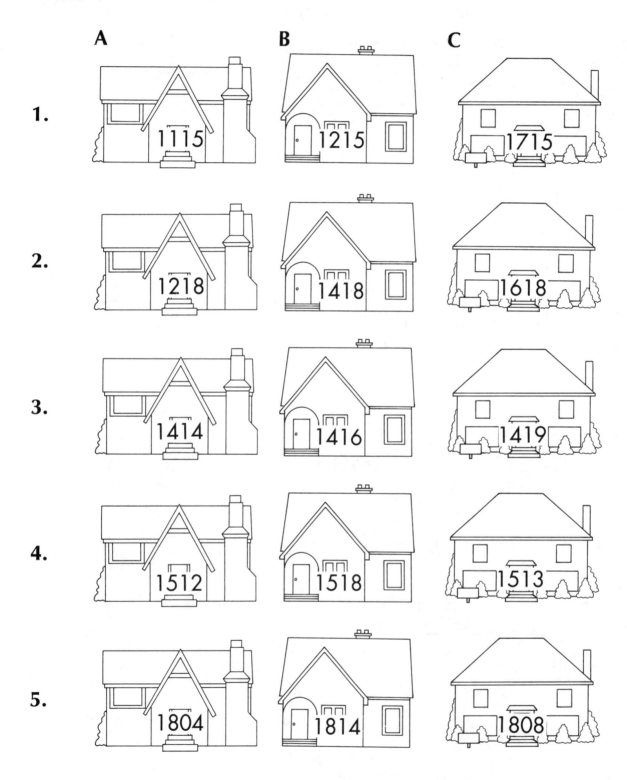

1. 1115   1215   1715

2. 1218   1418   1618

3. 1414   1416   1419

4. 1512   1518   1513

5. 1804   1814   1808

8

	A	B	C
6.	1104	1111	1107
7.	1002	1012	1003
8.	1708	1718	1728
9.	2303	1323	2313
10.	2717	1727	2707

PART 2

1. _____
2. _____
3. _____
4. _____
5. _____

6. _____
7. _____
8. _____
9. _____
10. _____

PRACTICE

PART 1

1	2	3	4	5	6	7	8	9	10	11	12	13
A	B	C	D	E	F	G	H	I	J	K	L	M

14	15	16	17	18	19	20	21	22	23	24	25	26
N	O	P	Q	R	S	T	U	V	W	X	Y	Z

PART 2

PART 3

UNIT 2 MONEY AND TIME

PRACTICE A

PART 1

A	B	C	D	E	F	G	H	I	J
10	20	30	40	50	60	70	80	90	100

PART 2

10+10=20

	A	B	C
1.	30	40	50
2.	40	60	80
3.	80	90	100
4.	40	50	60
5.	40	50	60
6.	80	90	100
7.	90	100	50
8.	60	80	70
9.	60	90	80
10.	100	90	70

PRACTICE B

PART 1

	A	B	C
1.	25	35	45
2.	65	75	25
3.	15	55	45
4.	35	85	95
5.	95	65	25
6.	15+55	15+45	15+65
7.	25+95	25+75	25+35
8.	65+25	65+85	65+45
9.	25+15	15+35	15+25
10.	75+25	35+75	25+75

PART 2

$$5+15=20$$

	A	B	C
1.	20	25	30
2.	20	25	30
3.	40	45	50
4.	40	45	50
5.	55	60	65
6.	55	60	65
7.	70	75	80
8.	70	75	80
9.	85	90	95
10.	85	90	95

PRACTICE C

PART 1

A	B	C	D

PART 2

	A	B	C
1.			
2.			
3.			
4.			
5.			

	A	**B**	**C**
6.			
7.			
8.			
9.			
10.			

PART 3

	A	**B**	**C**	**D**

PART 4

	A	B	C
1.			
2.			
3.			
4.			
5.			
6.			
7.			
8.			

PART 5

	A	B	C
1.	5¢	10¢	15¢
2.	5¢	10¢	15¢
3.	10¢	20¢	30¢
4.	10¢	20¢	30¢
5.	15¢	25¢	50¢
6.	15¢	25¢	50¢
7.	15¢	25¢	50¢
8.	10¢	20¢	30¢
9.	25¢	50¢	75¢
10.	25¢	50¢	75¢
11.	10¢	15¢	25¢
12.	7¢	12¢	21¢
13.	15¢	20¢	25¢
14.	20¢	25¢	30¢
15.	32¢	27¢	35¢
16.	50¢	60¢	70¢
17.	55¢	60¢	70¢
18.	70¢	75¢	80¢
19.	75¢	80¢	85¢
20.	40¢	50¢	90¢

PRACTICE D

PART 1

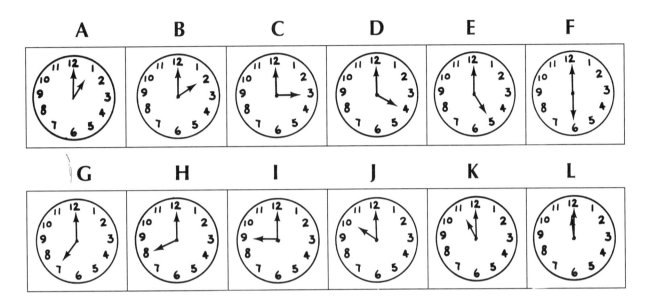

PART 2

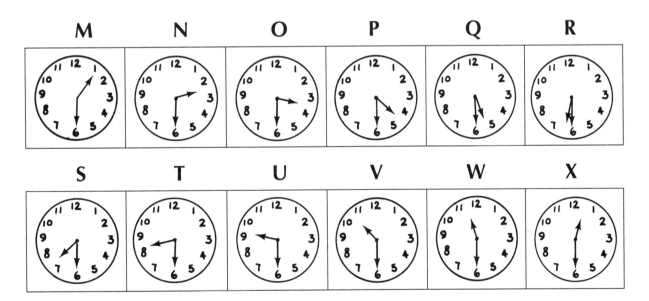

PART 3

	A	B	C
1.			
2.			
3.			
4.			
5.			
6.			
7.			
8.			
9.			
10.			
11.			
12.			

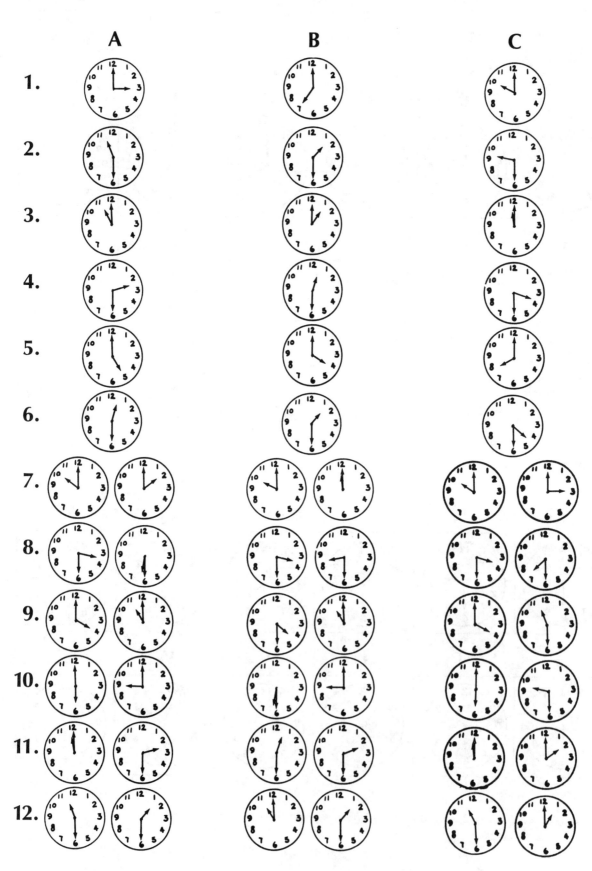

PRACTICE E

PART 1

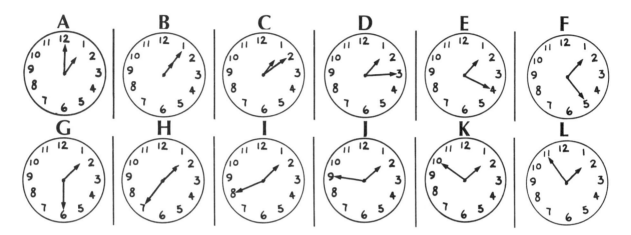

PART 2

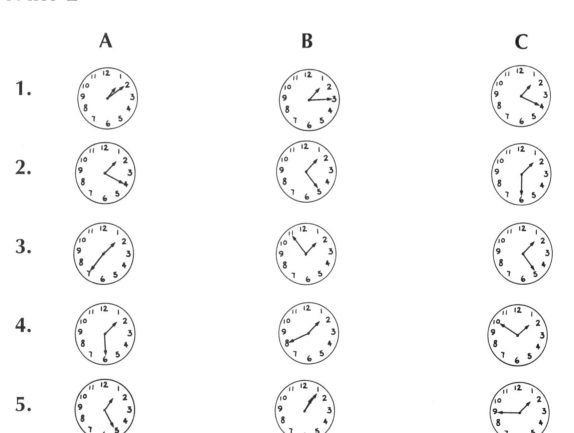

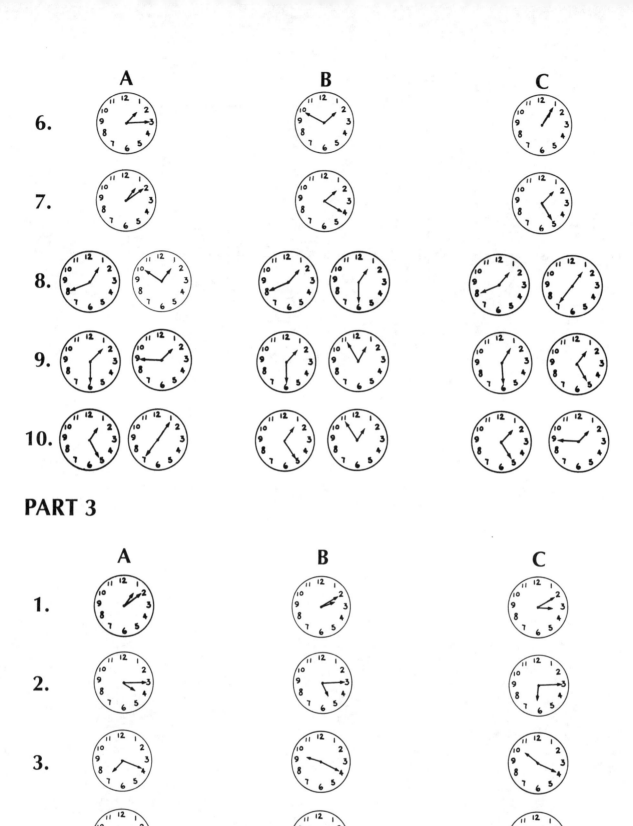

	A	B	C
6.			
7.			
8.			
9.			
10.			

PART 3

	A	B	C
1.			
2.			
3.			
4.			
5.			

	A	B	C

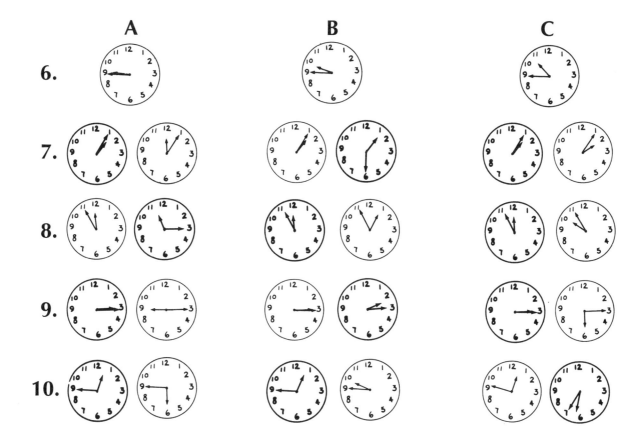

6.

7.

8.

9.

10.

PRACTICE F

PART 1

A	B	C	D	E	F

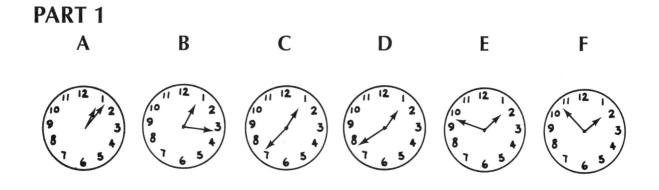

PART 2

	A	B	C
1.			
2.			
3.			
4.			
5.			
6.			
7.			
8.			
9.			
10.			

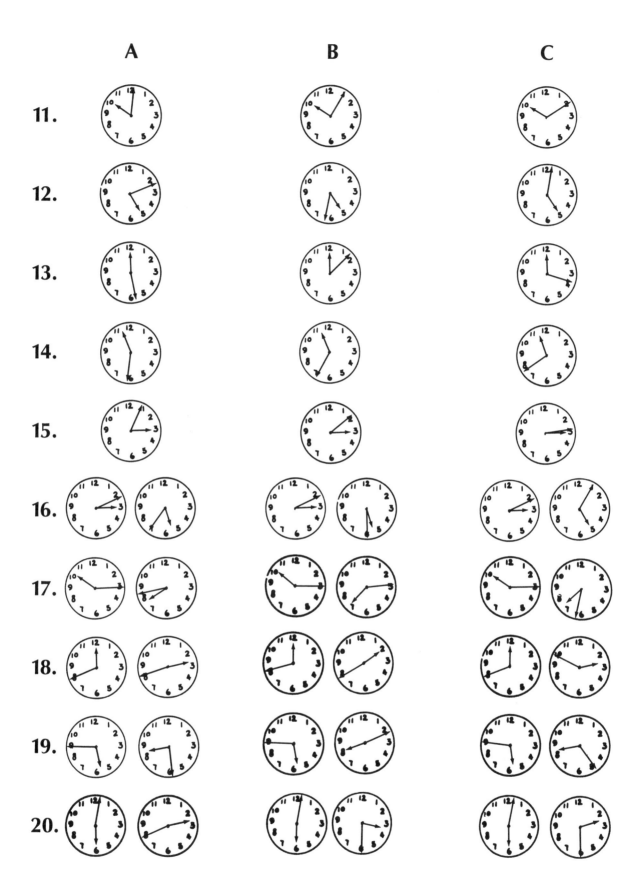

PART 3

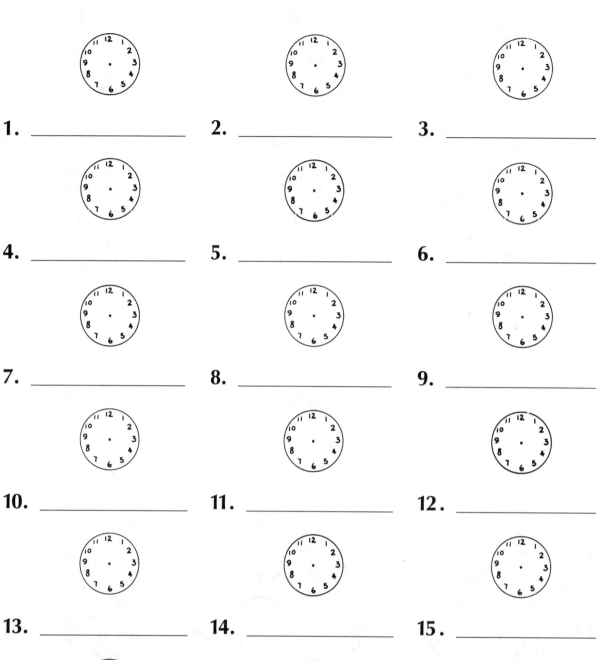

1. _____

2. _____

3. _____

4. _____

5. _____

6. _____

7. _____

8. _____

9. _____

10. _____

11. _____

12. _____

13. _____

14. _____

15. _____

16. _____

17. _____

18. _____

19. _____

20. _____

UNIT 3

CLOTHES AND THINGS

PRESENTATION A

1.

2.

3.

4.

5.

6.

7.

8.

9.

PRACTICE A

	A	B	C
1.			
2.			
3.			
4.			
5.			

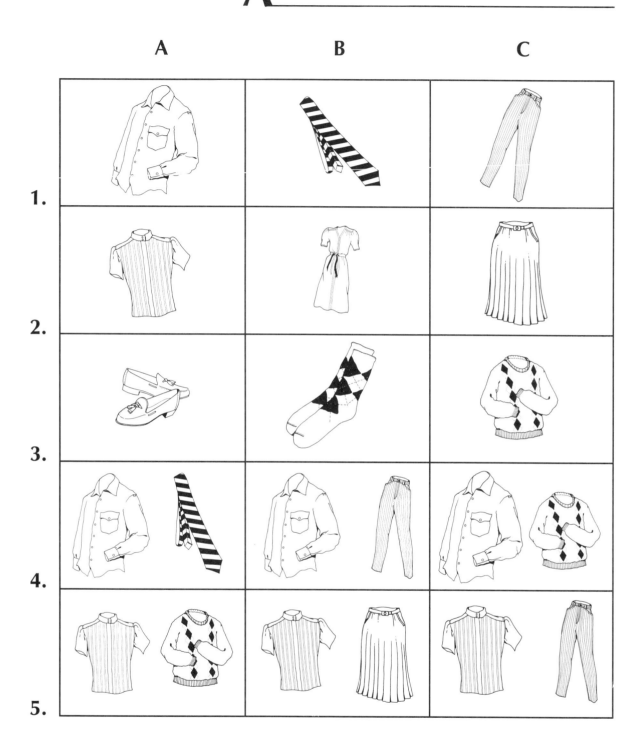

27

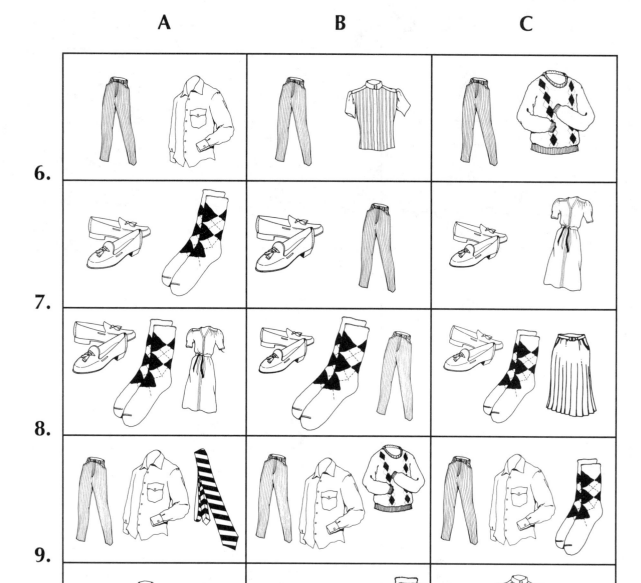

A   B   C

6.

7.

8.

9.

10.

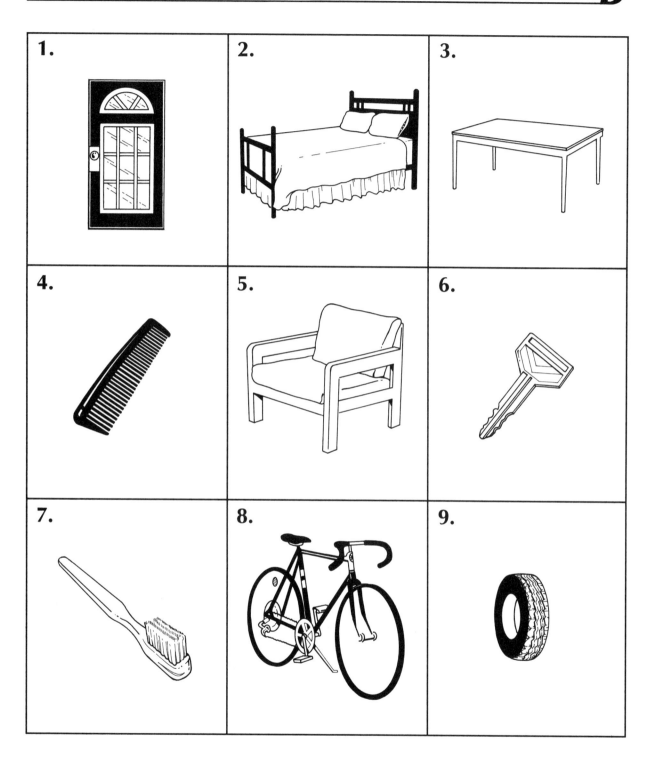

	A	B	C
1.			
2.			
3.			
4.			

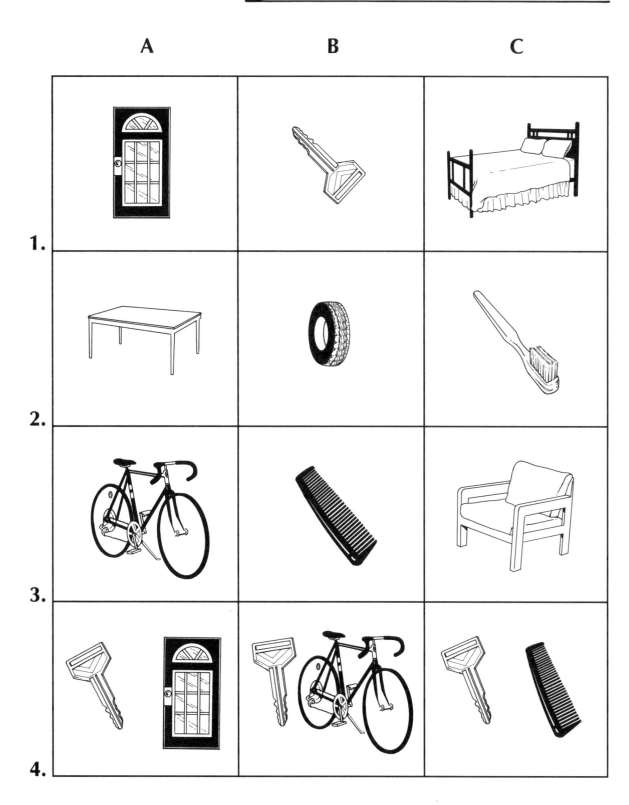

	A	**B**	**C**
5.			
6.			
7.			
8.			
9.			

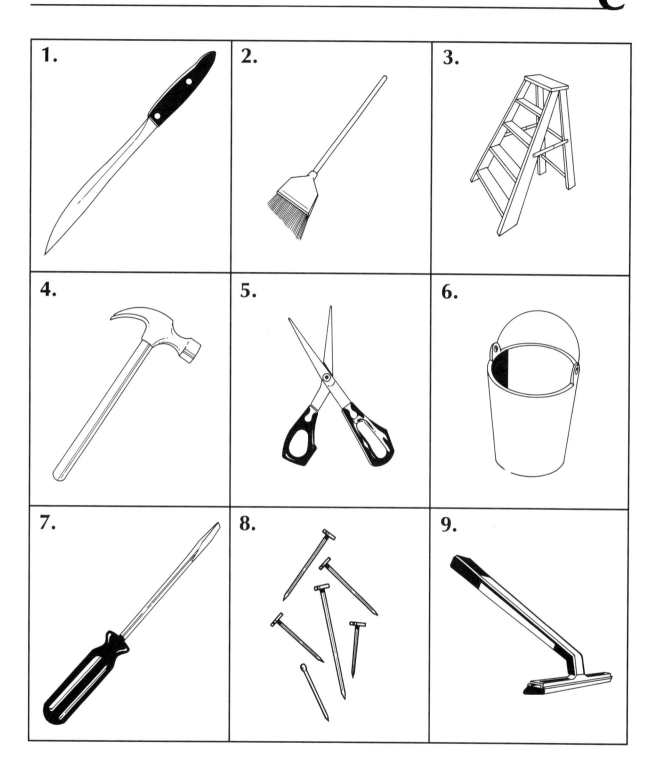

1.

2.

3.

4.

5.

6.

7.

8.

9.

	A	B	C

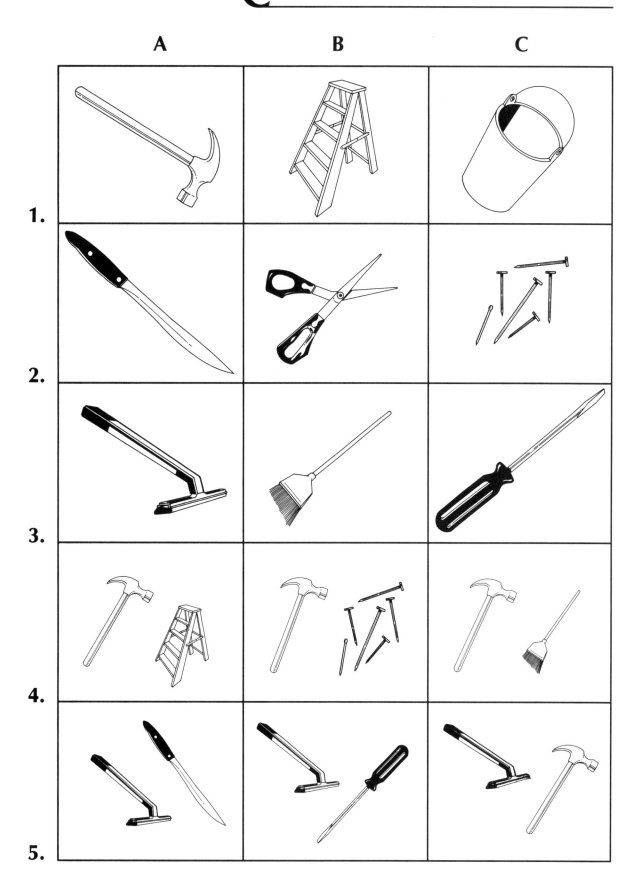

	A	B	C
6.			
7.			
8.			
9.			
10.			

36

1. Tie
2. Key
3. Bed
4. Tire
5. Door
6. Comb
7. Nails
8. Socks
9. Knife
10. Dress
11. _____
12. Table

13. <u>s h i r t</u>

14. _ _ _ _ _ _

15. _ _ _ _ _ _

16. <u>b r o o m</u>

17. <u>s h i r t</u>

18. <u>s h o e s</u>

19. _ _ _ _ _ _ _

20 _ _ _ _ _ _ _

21. <u>h a m m e r</u>

22. _ _ _ _ _ _ _

23. <u>b i c y c l e</u>

24. <u>s w e a t h e r</u>

25. <u>s c i s s o r s</u>

26. <u>t o o t h b r u s h</u>

27. _ _ _ _ _ _ _ _ _ _

$99.95	$14.96	$1.09
$6.47	$47.50	$19.95
$3.33	$2.57	$1.88
$33.50	$1.78	$84.99

UNIT

THE BODY

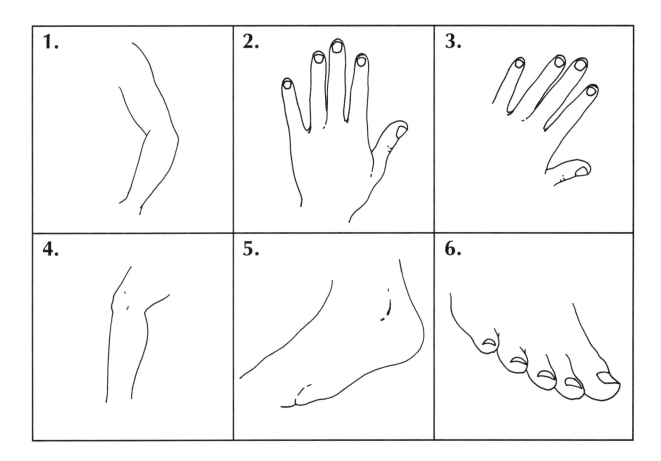

PRACTICE A

	A	B	C
1.			
2.			
3.			
4.			
5.			
6.			

43

	A	**B**	**C**
7.			
8.			
9.			
10.			
11.			
12.			

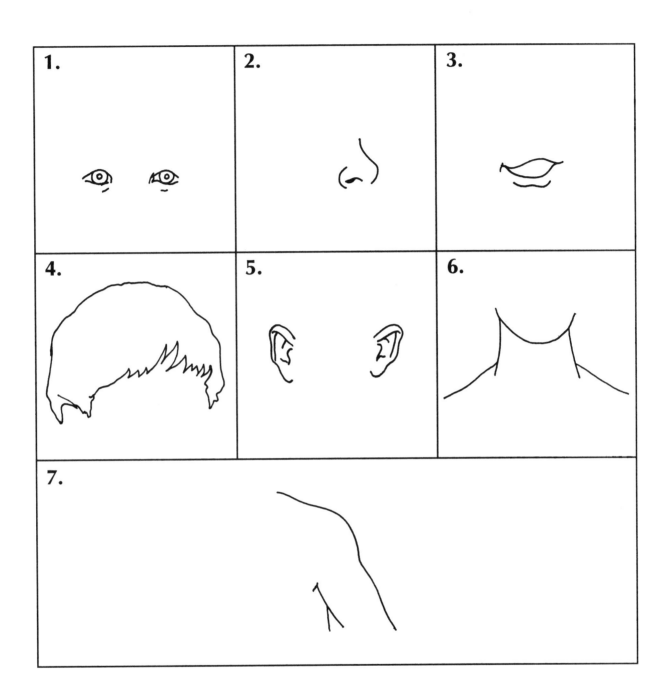

	A	B	C
1.			
2.			
3.			
4.			
5.			
6.			

	A	B	C
7.			
8.			
9.			
10.			
11.			
12.			

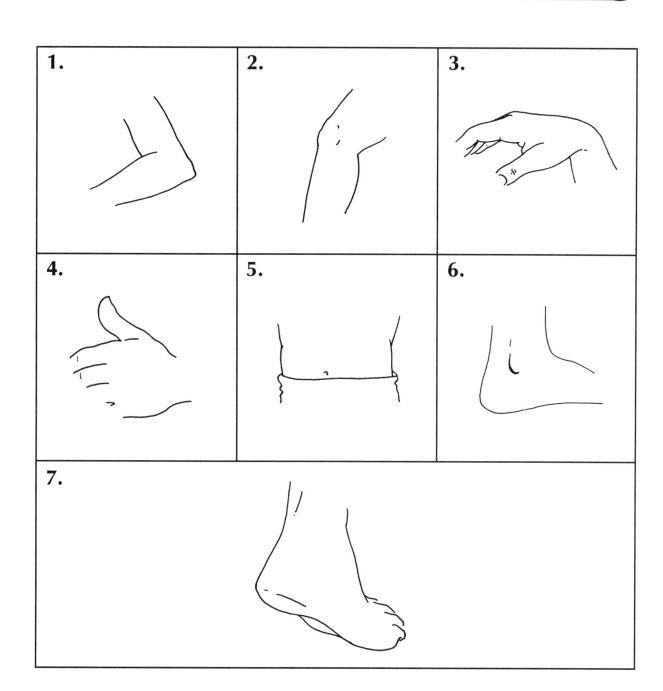

1.

2.

3.

4.

5.

6.

7.

PRACTICE C

	A	B	C
1.			
2.			
3.			
4.			
5.			
6.			

	A	B	C
7.			
8.			
9.			
10.			
11.			
12.			

PRACTICE D

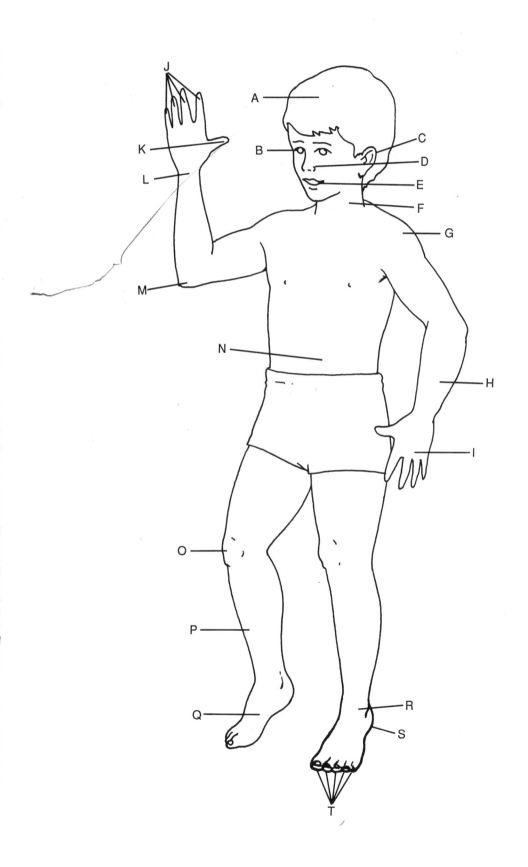

J 1. _D_____
P 2. _____
B 3. _____
H 4. _____
N 5. _____
I 6. _____
7 7. _____
D 8. _____
O 9. _____
R 10. _____
I 11. _____
C 12. _____
K 13. _____
Q 14. _____
G 15. _____
H 16. _____
S 17. _____
F 18. _____
L 19. _____
E 20. _____

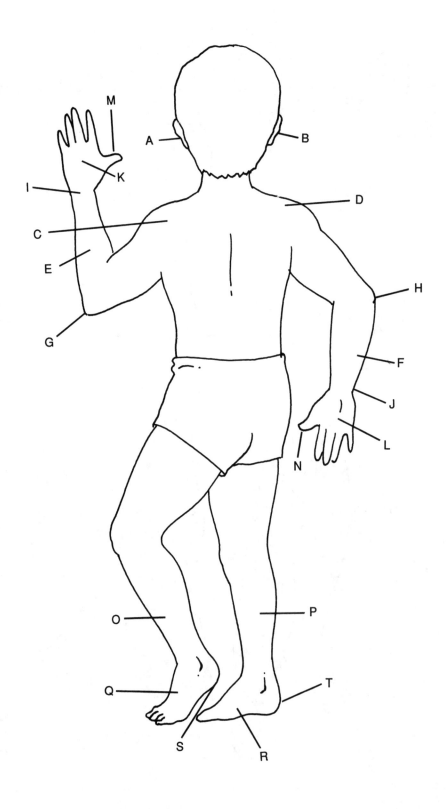

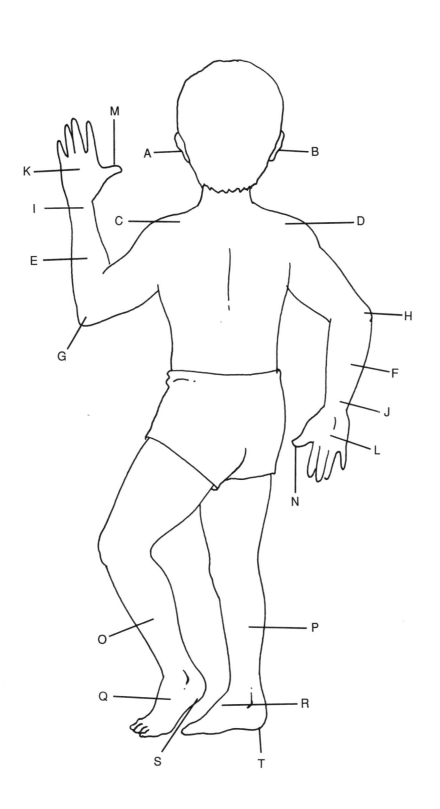

K 1. ____
R 2. ____
B 3. ____
O 4. ____
E 5. ____
H 6. ____
P 7. ____
D 8. ____
S 9. ____
F 10. ____
I 11. ____
N 12. ____
H 13. ____
C 14 ____
L 15. ____
A 16. ____
J 17. ____
Q 18. ____
G 19. ____
T 20. ____

UNIT

5 SHAPES

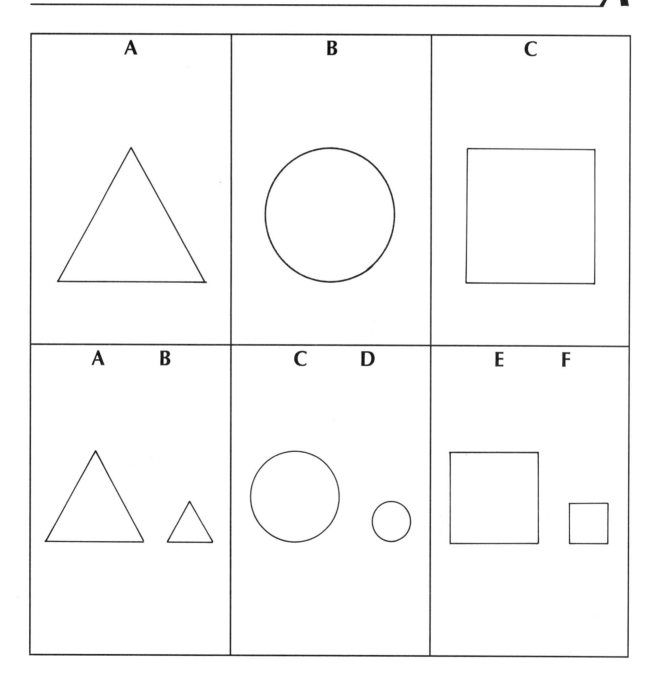

A	B	C

A B	C D	E F

	A	B	C
1.	○ o	○ □	○ △
2.	△ △	△ □	△ o
3.	□ △	□ □	□ o
4.	○ □ △	○ □ △	o □ △
5.	□ o △	□ ○ △	□ ○ △
6.	△ △ o	△ △ ○	△ △ o
7.	○ □ ○	○ □ ○	○ □ o
8.	□ □ △ ○	□ □ △ o	□ □ △ o
9.	△ △ △ □ ○	△ △ △ □ o	△ △ △ □ ○
10.	o o o □ △	o o o □ △	o o o □ △
11.	△ △ □ □ □	△ △ □ □ □	△ △ □ □ □
12.	△ o o o □	△ ○ ○ ○ □	△ o o o △
13.	○ ○ □ □ △	○ ○ □ □ △	○ ○ □ □ △
14.	○ o □ □ △	○ o □ □ △	○ ○ □ □ △
15.	□ □ □ ○ o △	□ □ ○ ○ o △	□ □ □ o ○ △

A	B	C	D	E

PRACTICE B

1.

2.

3.

4.

5.

	A	**B**	**C**

6.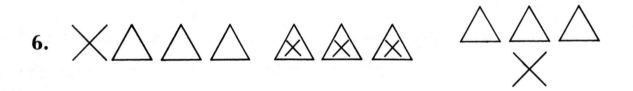

7.

8.

9.

10.

1.

2.

3.

4.

5.

UNIT
6 DOING THINGS

1.
2.
3.
4.
5.
6.
7.
8.
9.

PRACTICE A

	A	B	C
1.			
2.			
3.			
4.			
5.			
6.			
7.			

	A	**B**	**C**
8.			
9.			
10.			
11.			
12.			
13.			
14.			
15.			

A.

B.

C.

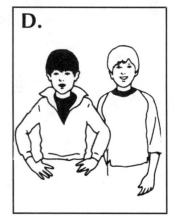
D.

PRACTICE **B**

PART 1

	A	B
1.		
2.		
3.		

	A	**B**

4.

5.

6.

7.

8.

9.

PART 2

A   B

1.

2.

3.

4.

5.

6.

7.

8.

PART 3

	A	**B**	**C**

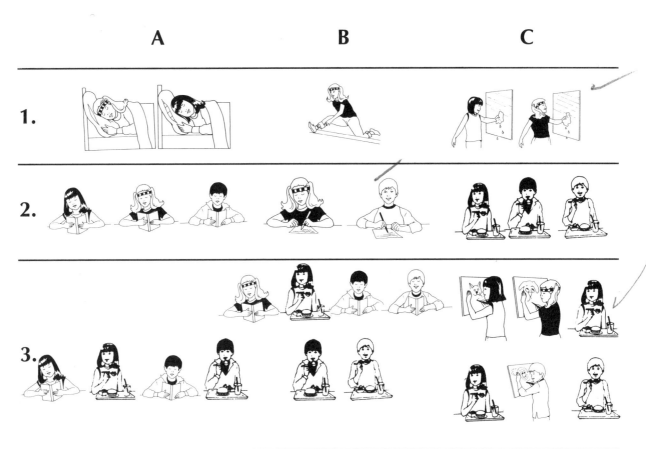

1.

2.

3.

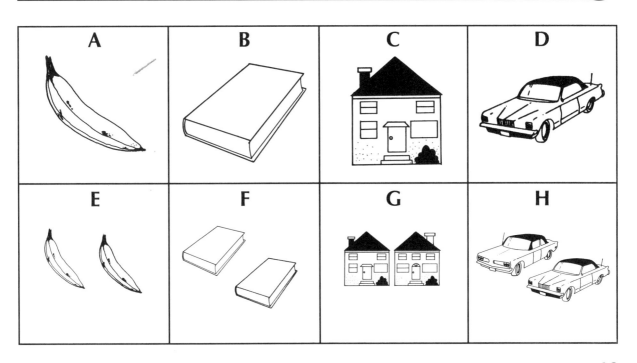

A	**B**	**C**	**D**
E	**F**	**G**	**H**

PRACTICE C

PART 1

	A	B
1.		
2.		
3.		
4.		
5.		

PART 2

	A	B	C	
1.				
2.				
3.				
4.				
5.				

PART 3

	A	**B**	**C**
1.			
2.			
3.	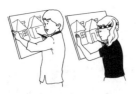		
4.			

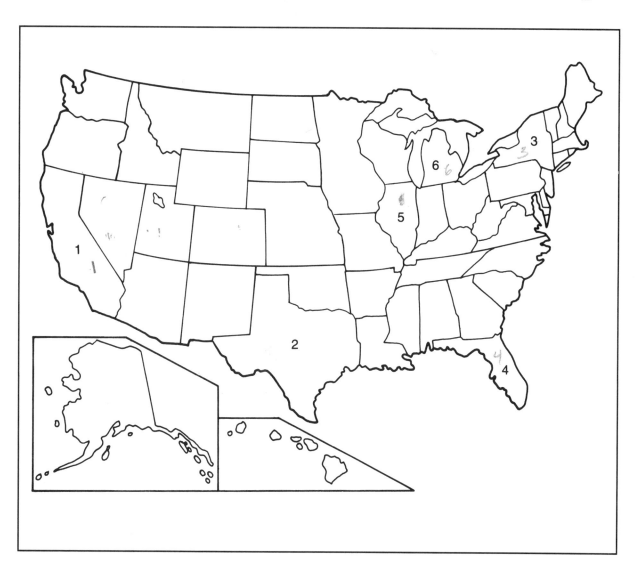

	A	B	C

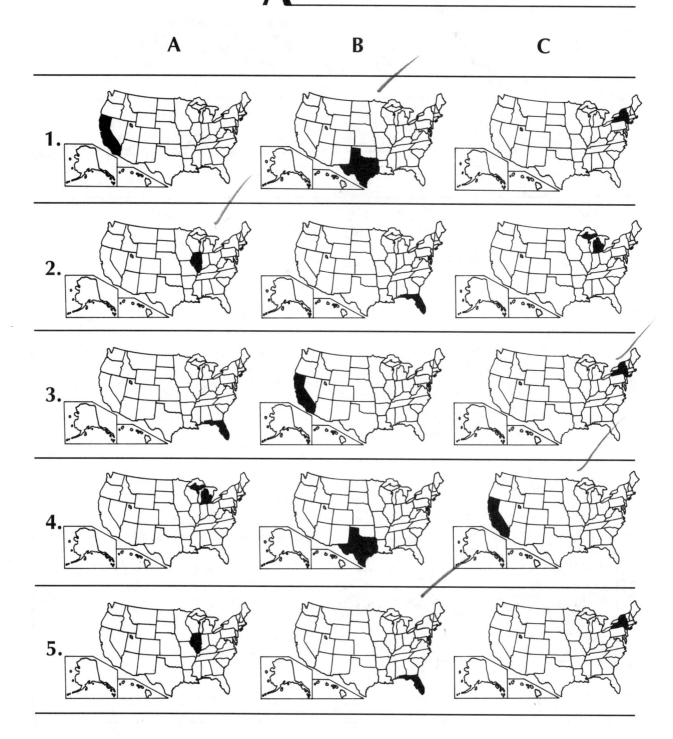

1. 2. 3. 4. 5.

A   B   C

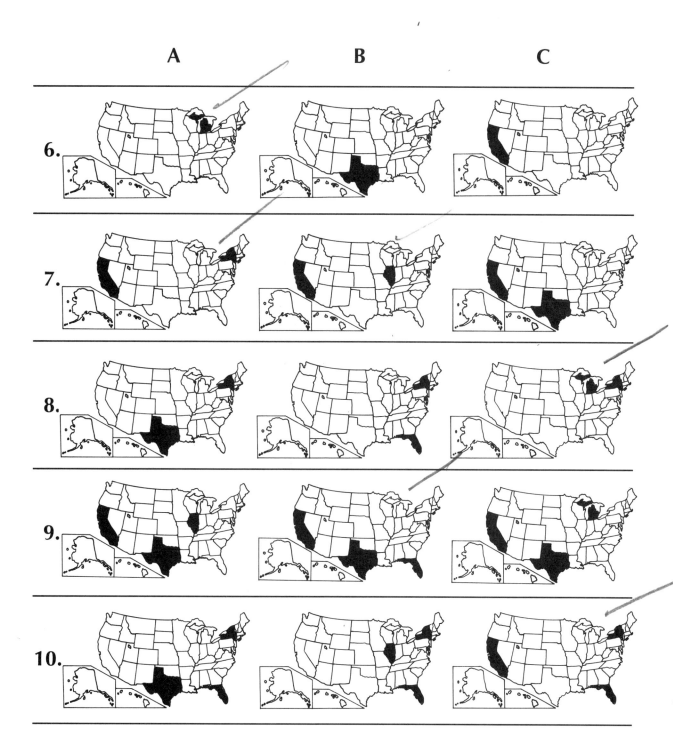

6.

7.

8.

9.

10.

75

PRACTICE B

	A	B	C

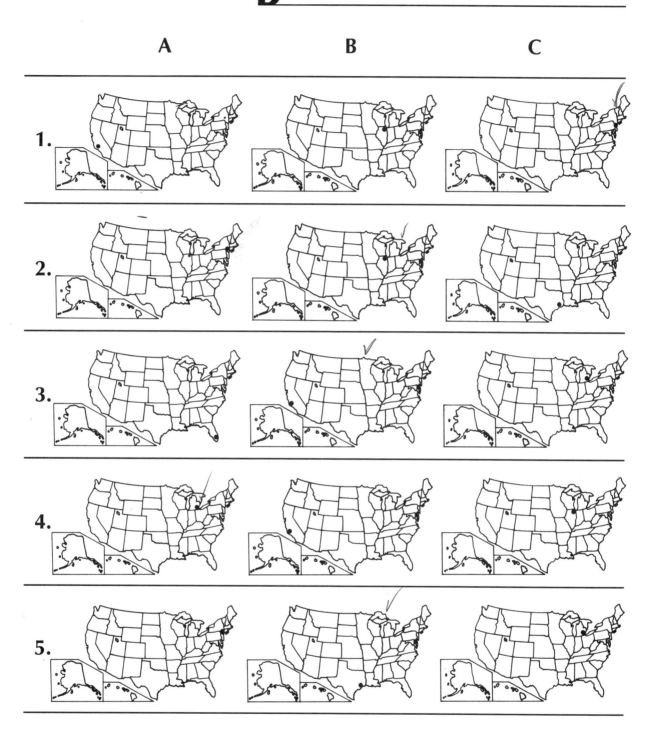

1.
2.
3.
4.
5.

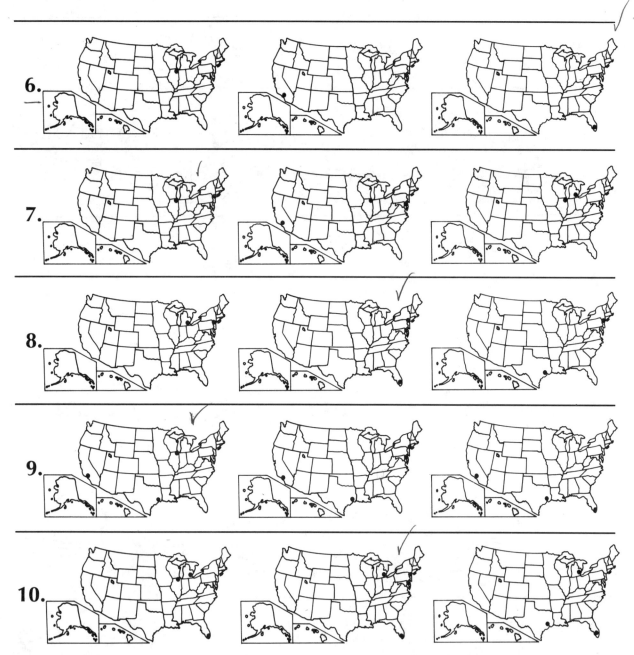

6.

7.

8.

9.

10.

A	B	C	D	E	F	G	H	I	
100	200	300	400	500	600	700	800	900	
J	K	L	M	N	O	P	Q	R	S
1,000	2,000	3,000	4,000	5,000	6,000	7,000	8,000	9,000	10,000
AA	BB	CC	DD	EE	FF	GG	HH	II	
110	120	130	140	150	160	170	180	190	
JJ	KK	LL	MM	NN	OO	PP	QQ	RR	
1,100	1,200	1,300	1,400	1,500	1,600	1,700	1,800	1,900	

PRACTICE *C*

PART 1

	A	B	C
1.	100	1,000 ✓	1,100
2.	1,100	1,010	1,110
3.	1,010	1,110 ✓	1,001
4.	150	1,500	1,050 ✓
5.	1,005 ✓	1,055	1,500
6.	4,404 ✓	4,044	4,040
7.	6,600	6,016 ✓	6,066
8.	8,800 ✓	8,080	8,808
9.	7,017	7,770	7,707 ✓
10.	9,099 ✓	9,999	9,909

PART 2

1. 1,214
2. 4,782
3. 9,949
4. 7304
5. 6,870

6. 2563
7. 5655
8. 3116
9. 8412
10. 10728

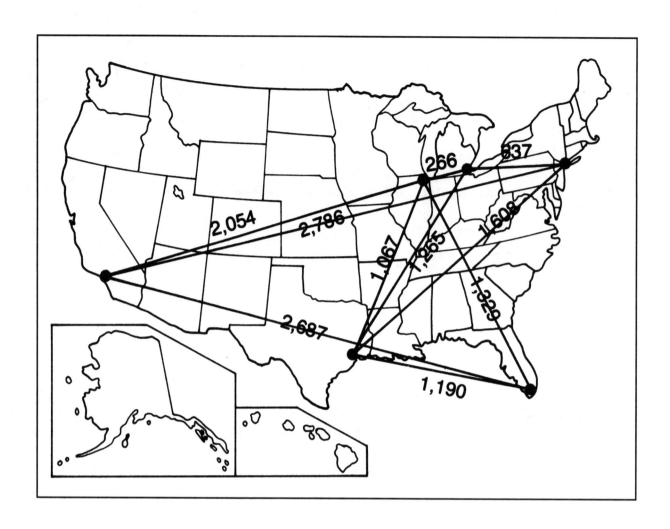

PRACTICE D

1. 2,054   MIS
2. 1,190   MIS
3. 6.37   MIS
4. 2.687   MIS
5. 12.65   MIS

6. 2.786   MIS
7. 1.608   MIS
8. 1.329   MIS
9. 266   MIS
10. 1,067   MIS

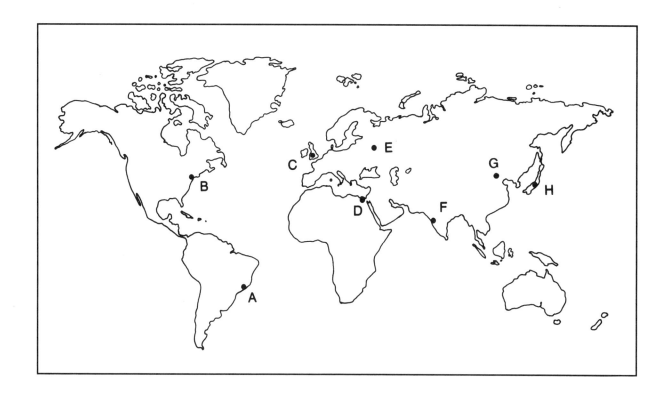

A	B	C	D	E
10,000	20,000	30,000	40,000	50,000

F	G	H	I
60,000	70,000	80,000	90,000

PRACTICE E

PART 1

	A	B	C
1.	110	1,010	10,000
2.	1,010	10,000	10,100
3.	11,000	10,111	11,100
4.	12,020	12,200	12,202
5.	14,014	14,400	14,140
6.	50,505	55,500	50,050
7.	77,017	77,707	70,777
8.	80,880	80,080	88,808
9.	90,990	90,999	90,019

PART 2

1. _____
2. _____
3. _____
4. _____
5. _____

6. _____
7. _____
8. _____
9. _____
10. _____

A	B	C	D	E
100,000	200,000	300,000	400,000	500,000
F	G	H	I	J
600,000	700,000	800,000	900,000	1,000,000
K	L	M	N	O
2,000,000	3,000,000	4,000,000	5,000,000	6,000,000
P	Q		R	S
7,000,000	8,000,000		9,000,000	10,000,000

PRACTICE F

PART 1

	A	B	C
1.	10,000	100,000	1,000,000
2.	101,000	1,100,000	1,010,000
3.	200,000	220,000	2,020,000
4.	3,000,300	3,300,000	3,030,000
5.	4,000,400	400,000	4,400,000
6.	7,070,000	7,000,070	7,770,000
7.	19,000,000	1,900,000	1,090,000
8.	24,000,000	2,400,000	2,024,000
9.	13,330,000	13,013,000	13,333,000
10.	14,400,000	14,040,000	114,440,000

PART 2

1. _____
2. _____
3. _____
4. _____
5. _____

6. _____
7. _____
8. _____
9. _____
10. _____

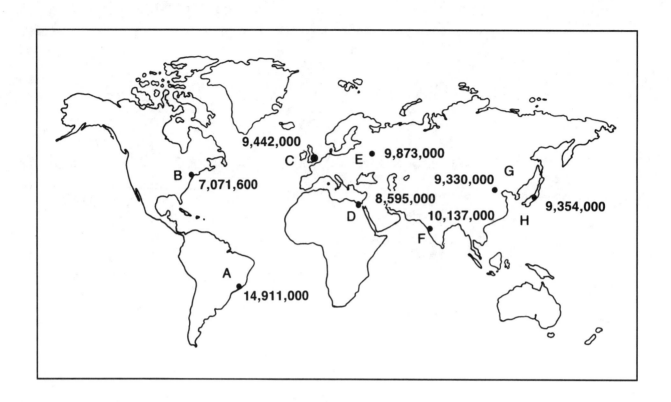

FOLLOW UP

1. _____
2. _____
3. _____
4. _____
5. _____
6. _____
7. _____
8. _____

UNIT

8 ASKING QUESTIONS

A.	**B.**	**C.**
D.	**E.**	**F.**
G.	**H.**	**I.**
J.	**K.**	**L.**
M.	**N.**	**O.**

PRACTICE A

	A	B	C

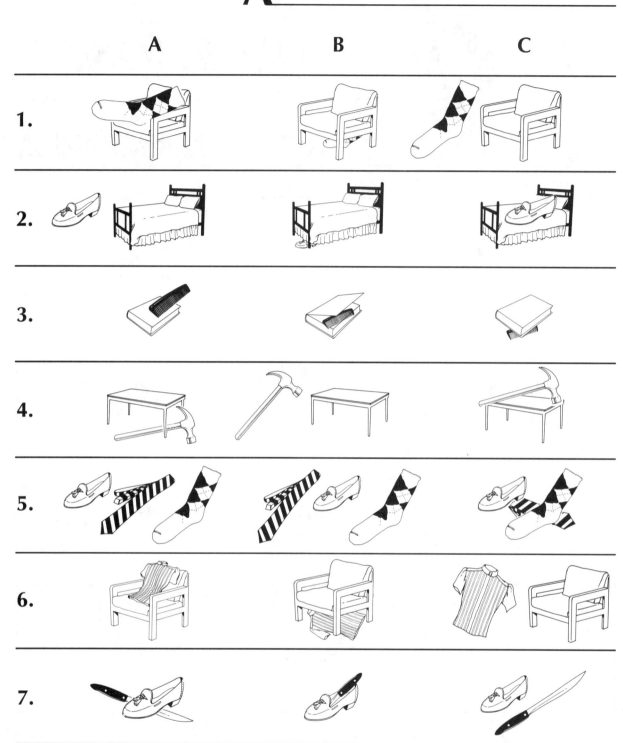

1.

2.

3.

4.

5.

6.

7.

	A	**B**	**C**

8.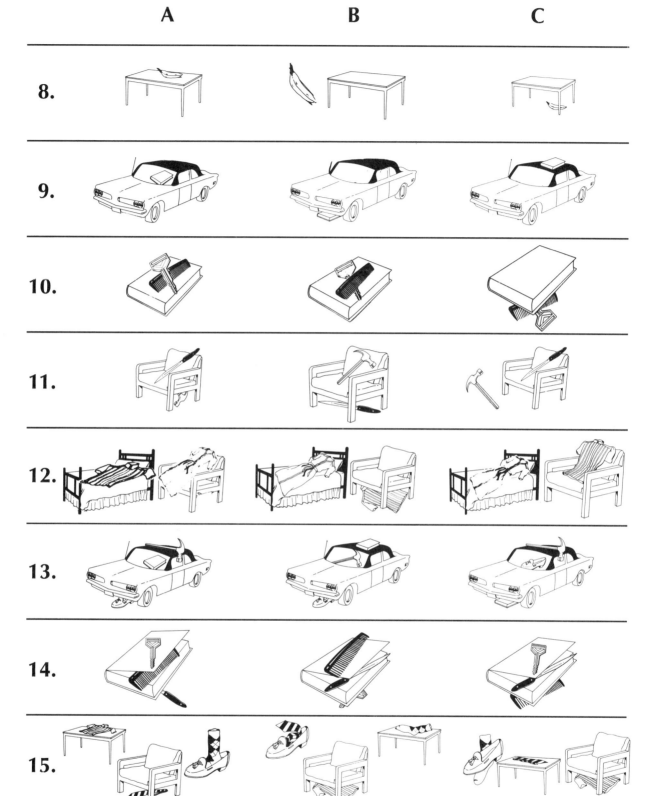

9.

10.

11.

12.

13.

14.

15.

PRACTICE B

	A	B	C

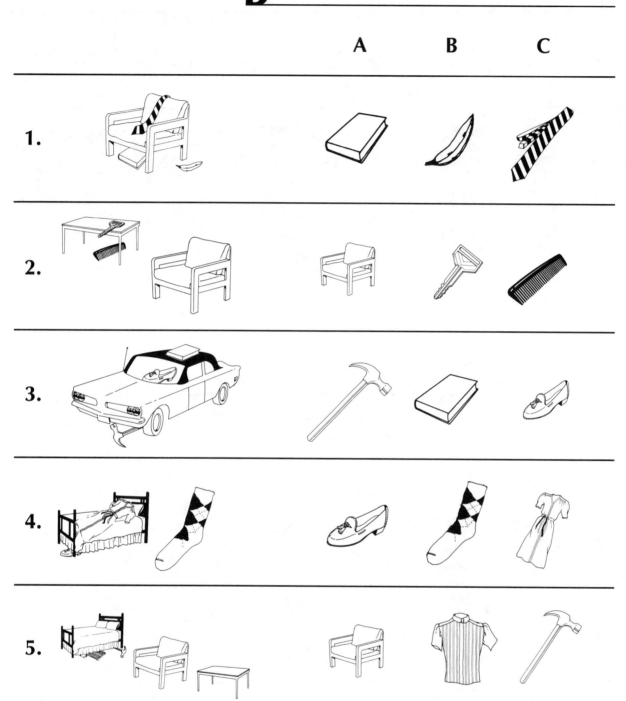

1.

2.

3.

4.

5.

6.

7.

8.

9.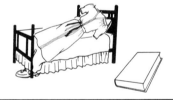

10.

PRACTICE D

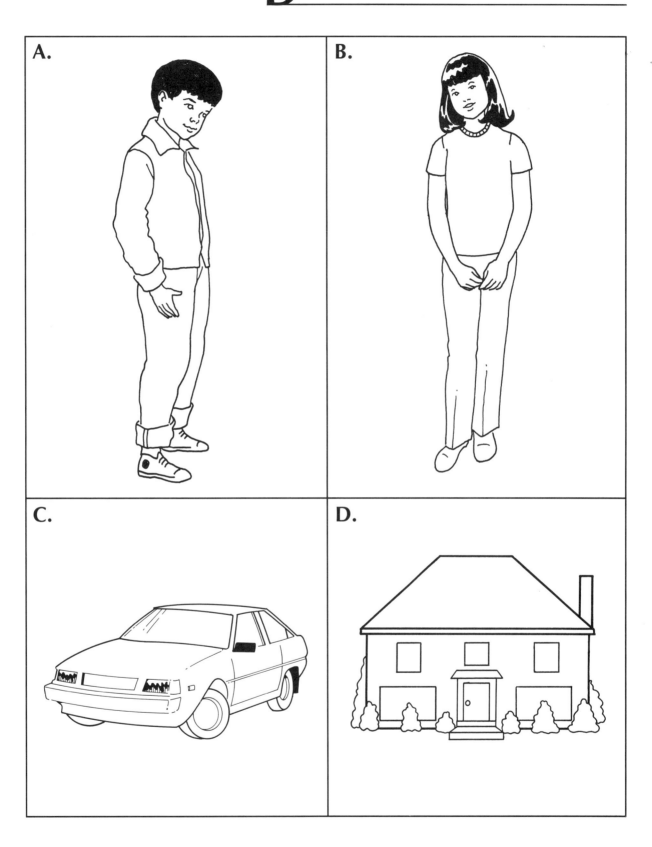

A.

B.

C.

D.

PRACTICE E

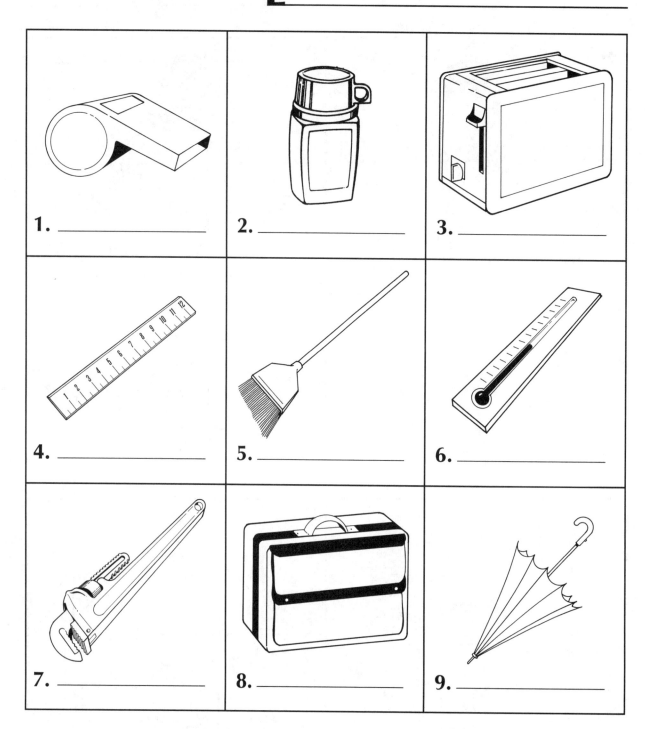

1. _____

2. _____

3. _____

4. _____

5. _____

6. _____

7. _____

8. _____

9. _____

A PPENDIX

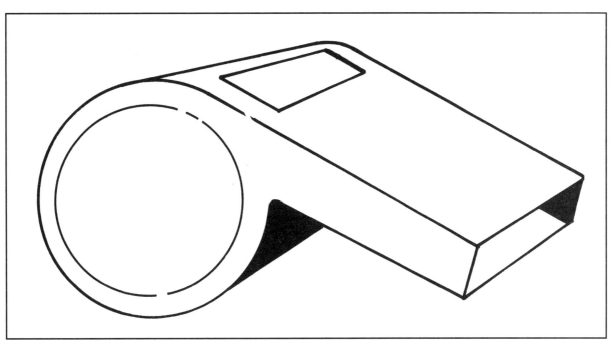

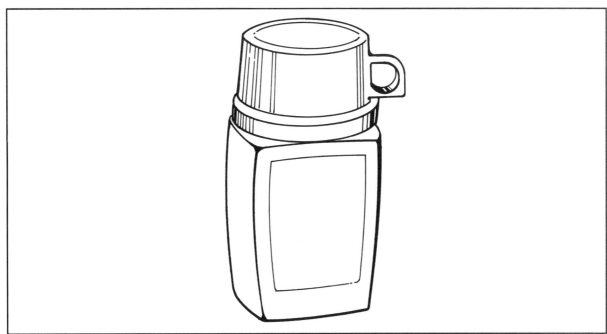

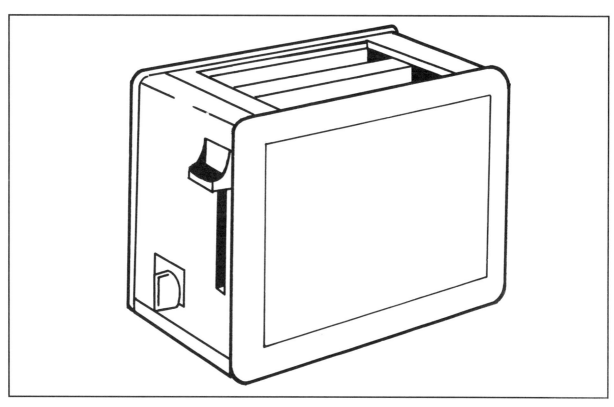

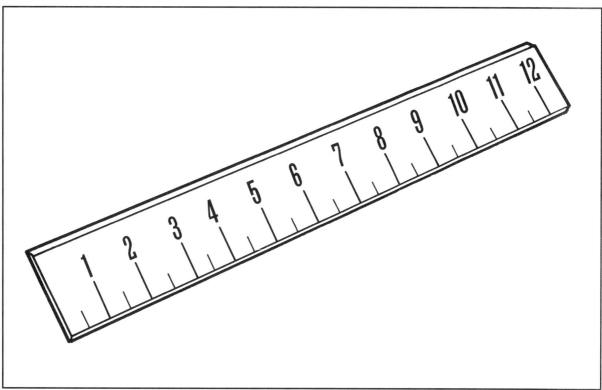

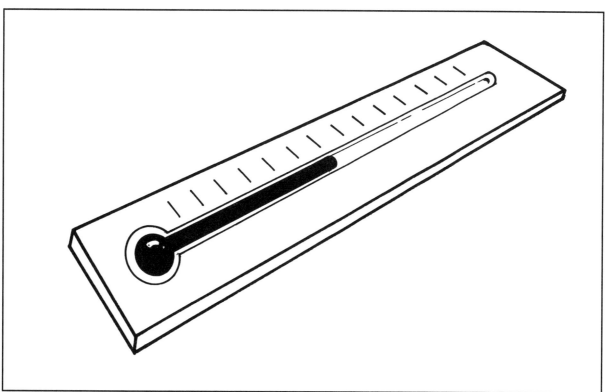

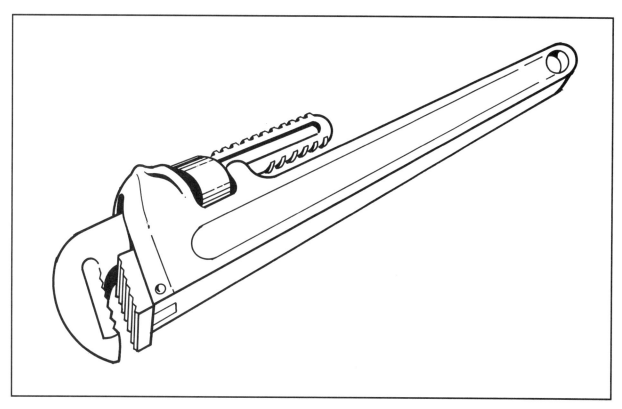

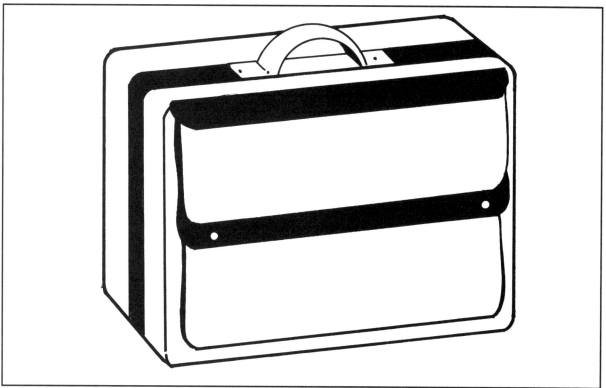

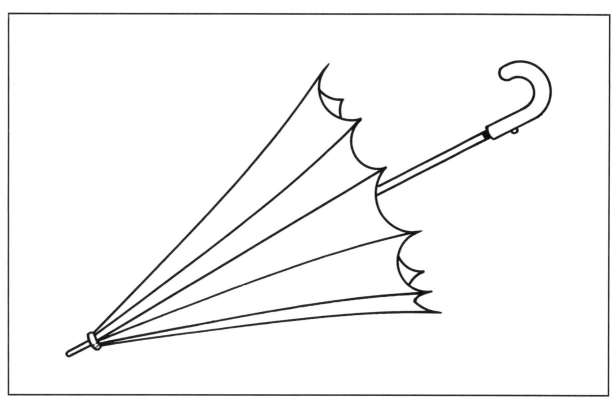

HOUSE

CAR

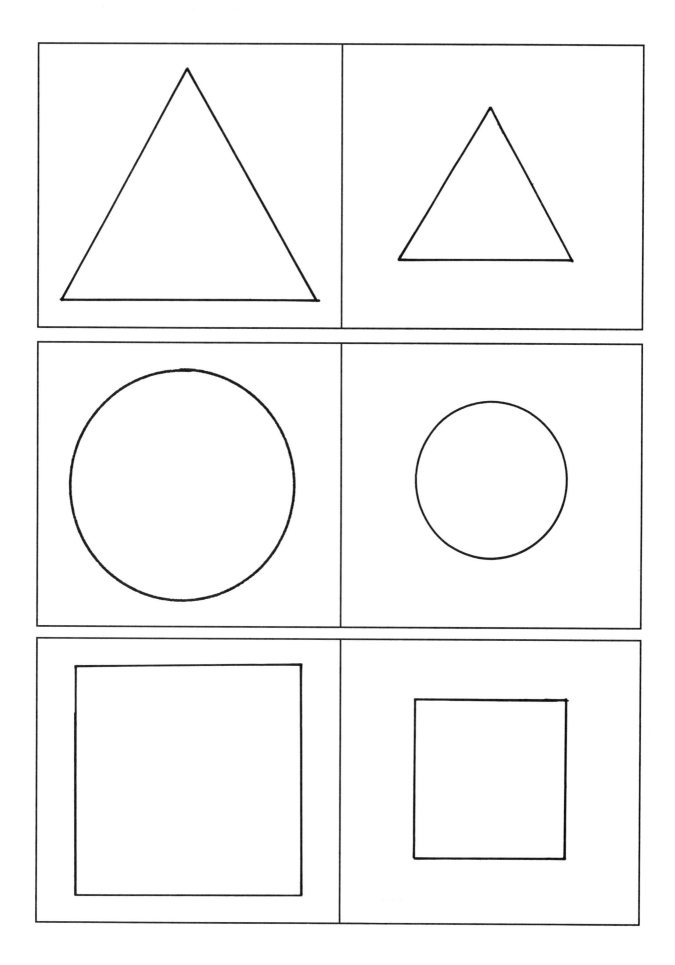

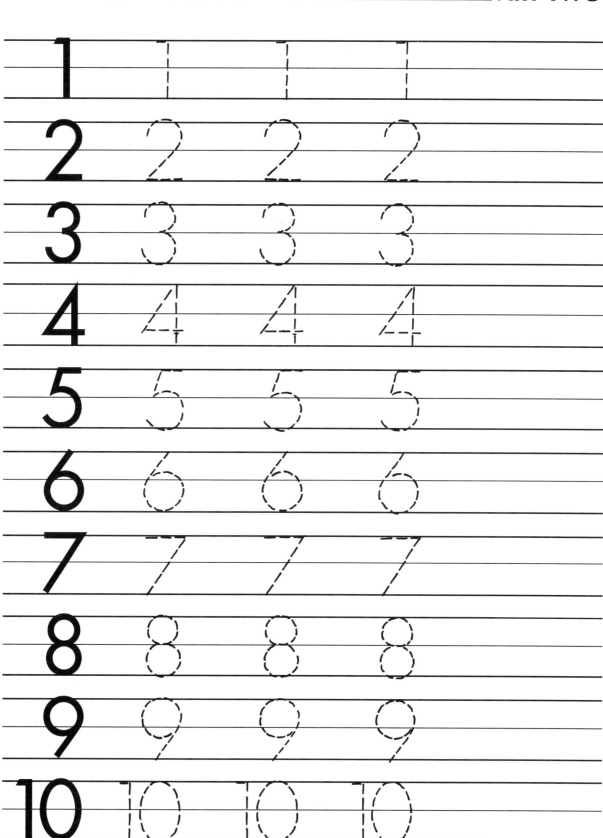

A A A A A

B B B B

C C C C

D D D D

E E E E

F F F F

G G G G

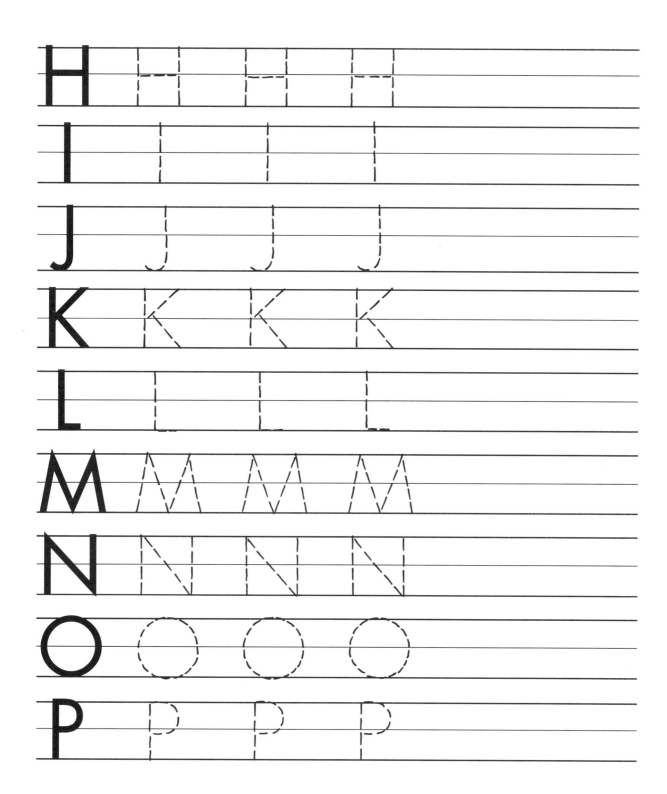

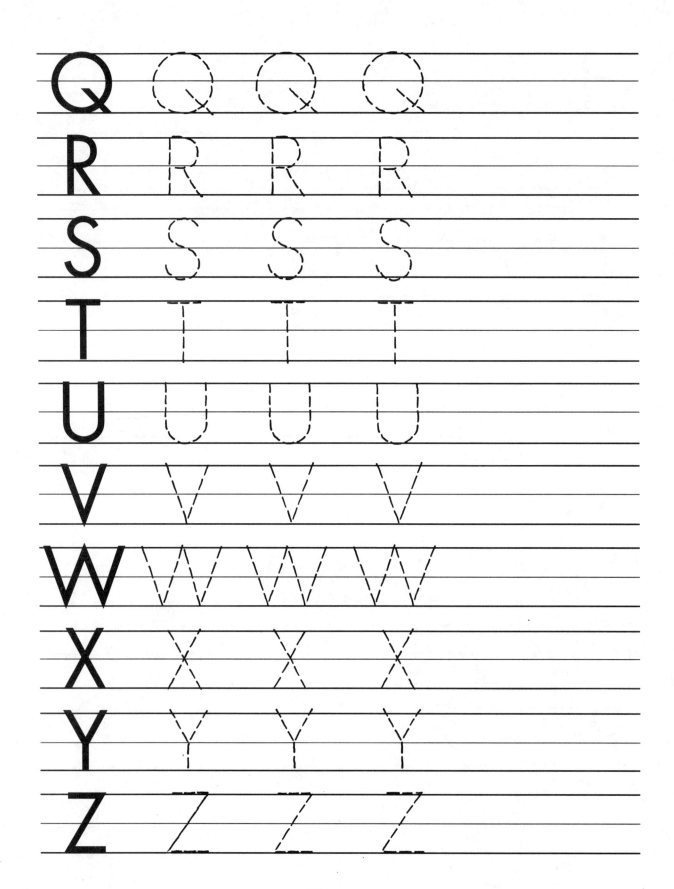